Merriam-Webster's Alphabet Book

WRITTEN AND ILLUSTRATED BY

Ruth Heller

Merriam-Webster, Incorporated
Springfield, Massachusetts, U.S.A.

Library of Congress Cataloging in Publication Data
Main entry under title:

Heller, Ruth.
   Merriam-Webster's alphabet book / written and illustrated by Ruth Heller.
      p. cm.
   ISBN-13: 978-0-87779-023-5 (hardcover : alk. paper)
   ISBN-10: 0-87779-023-X (hardcover : alk. paper)
   1. English language—Alphabet—Juvenile literature. I. Merriam-Webster, Inc.
II. Title.
   PE1155.H45 2005
428.1'3—dc22   2004029213

Made in the United States of America

123ID:QWV070605

Merriam-Webster's Alphabet Book

®

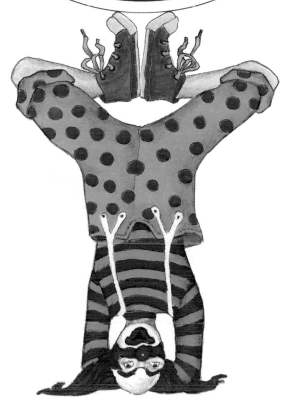

A
doesn't always sound the same.
In **April**, **May**, and **play**
and **game**,
it sounds exactly like its name,
but
has another sound in **fat**,
in
ant and **at** and **acrobat**,
and yet another sound in **all**,
in **also**, **walk**, and **talk** and **tall**.
We hear two different
sounds for **A**
in
alligator and **Saturday**.

B
has
one sound
and one alone
as in
blob,
balloon, and **bone**.
Sometimes though
it's in a word
where it is seen and
never heard.
In **crumb** and **climb**
and **doubt** and **lamb**,
B
is as silent as a clam.

C
sounds just like
the letter **K**
in **candy**, **picnic**,
clown, and **clay**.
It sounds like **S**
in **cent** and **dance**,
and has both sounds in
circumstance.
When **H**'s follow after **C**'s,
they make the sound
we hear in **cheese**.
Exceptions to
this rule are seen
in **Christopher**
and in **machine**.

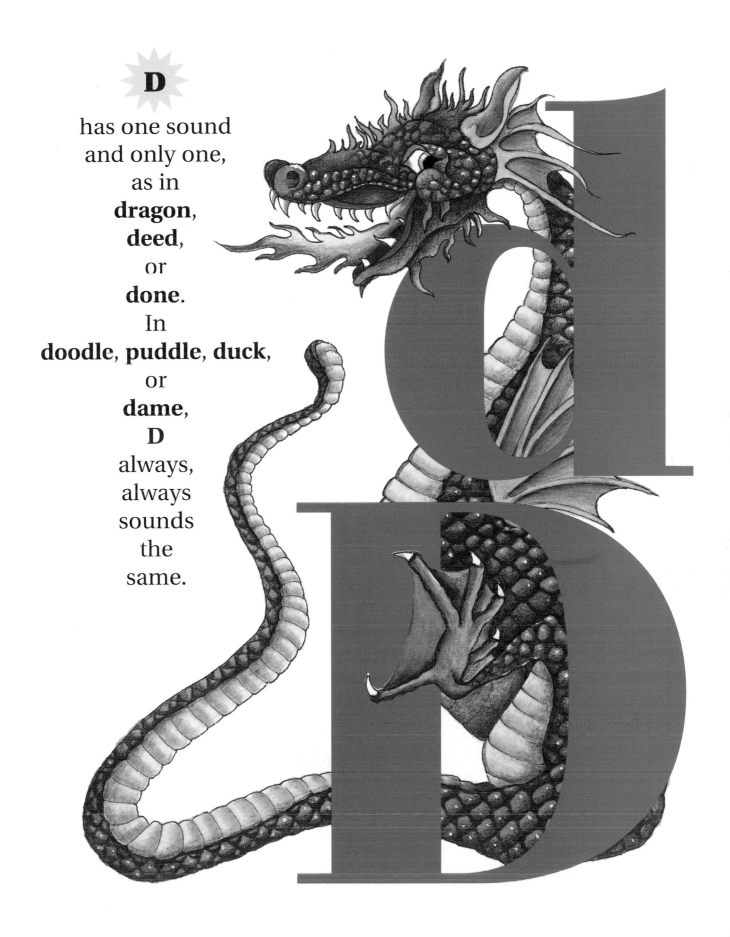

D
has one sound
and only one,
as in
dragon,
deed,
or
done.
In
doodle, **puddle**, **duck**,
or
dame,
D
always,
always
sounds
the
same.

E

has one sound in **Eskimo**,
in
messy, **shelf**, and **elf**.
In
equal, **Egypt**, **he**, and **she**,
it sounds just like itself.
Two sounds for
E
are in **retell** —
in
recess and **emcee**
as well.

F

has the sound we hear in **fluff**,
in **truffle**, **funny**, **frog**, and **stuff**.
But when we hear the **F** in **of**,
we hear a sound
that rhymes with
glove.

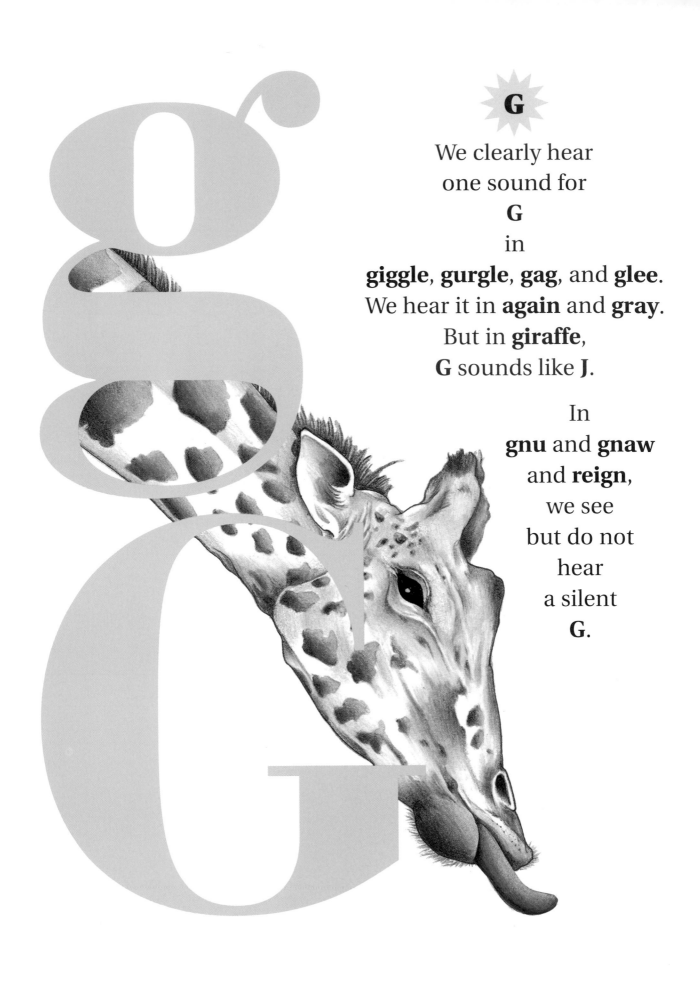

G

We clearly hear
one sound for
G
in
giggle, **gurgle**, **gag**, and **glee**.
We hear it in **again** and **gray**.
But in **giraffe**,
G sounds like **J**.

In
gnu and **gnaw**
and **reign**,
we see
but do not
hear
a silent
G.

H

has one sound
and it is found
in **hello**, **hoot**, and
hare and **hound**,
behave, **perhaps**,
and
him and **her**,
and in
heroic hamburger.
We hear the **H** in
hungry host,
but not in
honest, **hour**,
or **ghost**.

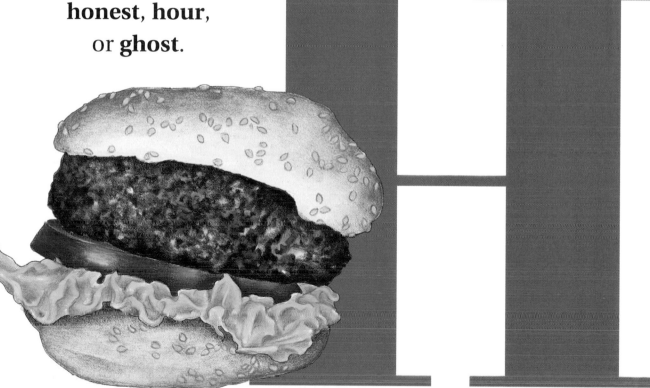

I

One sound for **I** is heard in
in,
in **insect**, **if**, and **itchy chin**.
It sounds just like its name in
ice,
in **slide** and **glide** and
mighty nice.
In **iodine** we hear it twice.
Each sound is heard in
width and **wide**,
and
both of them
are found **inside**.

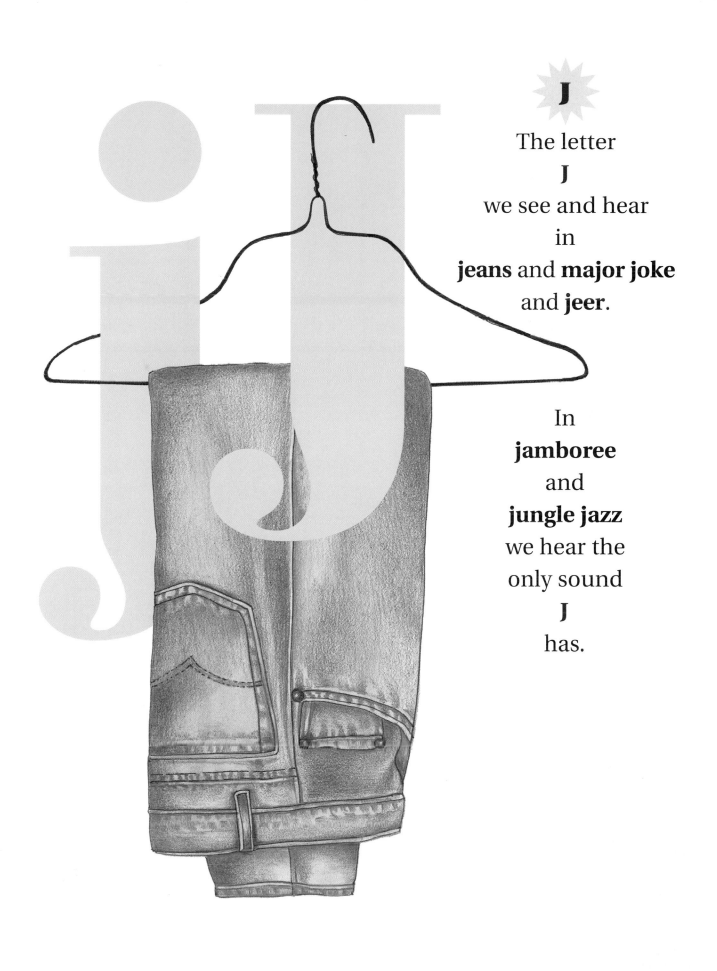

J

The letter
J
we see and hear
in
jeans and **major joke**
and **jeer**.

In
jamboree
and
jungle jazz
we hear the
only sound
J
has.

K

is heard in
king and **wink**,
koala, **kayak**,
kitchen sink.
It's heard in
twinkle,
sky, and **key**,
but is as silent
as can be
in
knuckle, **knight**,
and
knobby knee.

L

We hear the **L** in **leaf** and **ball**,
in
lollipop and **waterfall**,
in
lizards leap and **llamas loll**.
The sound of **L** is heard in **all**,
but
not in **stalk** and not in **half**
and
also not
in
chalk or **calf**.

M

has one sound
and
one alone,
as in
summer mumps
and
moan.
In
me and **my** and **mine**
and
them,
in **mask** and
meadow mouse
and **gem**,
we hear the only
sound
for **M**.

N
always, always
sounds the same.
In **noodle dinner**,
nibble, **name**,
in
neither, **nor**,
and
now
and
then,
in
nest
and
nightingale
and **wren**,
we hear
the only
sound for
N.
We see a silent **N**
in **column**,
hymn, and
autumn,
and in **solemn**.

O

One sound for
O
is heard in **no**,
in
clover, **open**, **close**, and **go**.
Another sound is heard in
hop,
in
octopus and **splotch** and
stop.
And yet another one in **who**,
in **whom** and **tomb** and
to and **do**.

October
has two sounds for
O,
and there are two in
domino.

P

The letter
P
has just one
sound,
as in
pepper, **parrot**,
pop, and **pound**.
When
H follows **P**
the sound will be
an **F**,
as in
photography.

Q
in front of **U** is seen
in
squish and **squash**
and
quake and **queen**.
U
almost always
follows
Q
and
sounds like
K with **W**.
Or else
it sounds
just like a
K,
as in
antique
or in **bouquet**.

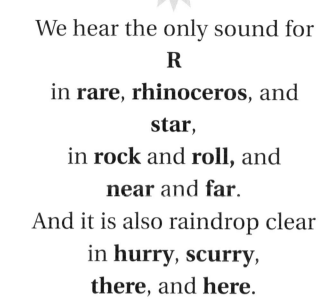

R

We hear the only sound for
R
in **rare**, **rhinoceros**, and
star,
in **rock** and **roll,** and
near and **far**.
And it is also raindrop clear
in **hurry**, **scurry**,
there, and **here**.

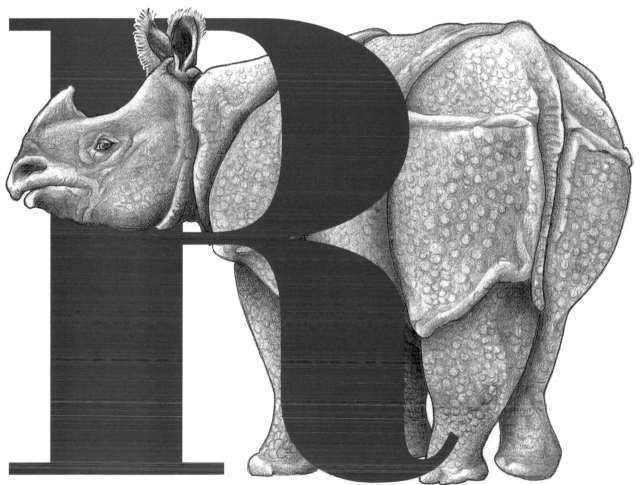

S

In
skeleton
and
fussy mess,
we clearly hear one
sound for **S**.
But **S**'s
sound the same as **Z**'s
in **music**, **easy**,
knees, and **peas**.
S and **H**
together make
the sound that's found
in **ship** and **shake**.
We clearly hear the **S**
in **smile**,
but not the one we see
in **isle**.

T

In **treasure**, **tattle**, **tale**, and **tree**,
we hear the one main sound for
T.
The sound in **that** and **those** and **thee**,
we hear when **H** comes after **T**.
A slightly different sound instead
is heard in **thick** and **thin**
and
thread.

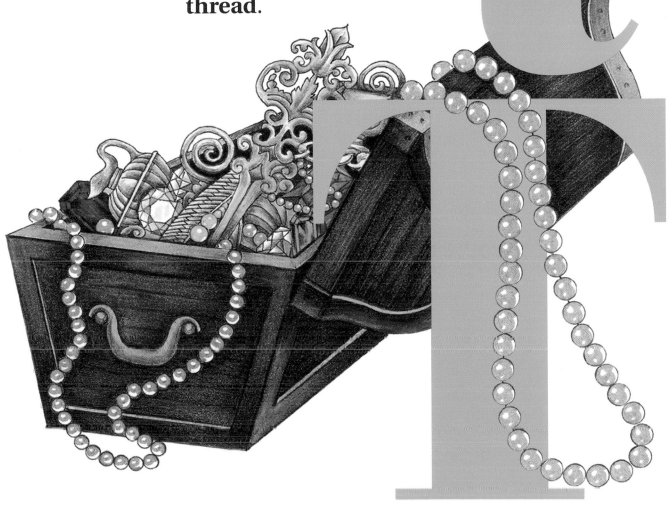

U

One sound for
U
is in **dispute**,
in **Utah**, **unicorn**, **compute**.
It
changes quite a bit in **bus**,
umbrella,
upper crust, and **us**.
It changes once again in **bush**,
in **bull**,
and **put** and **pull**
and **push**.
Two sounds for **U**
are in
unglue.

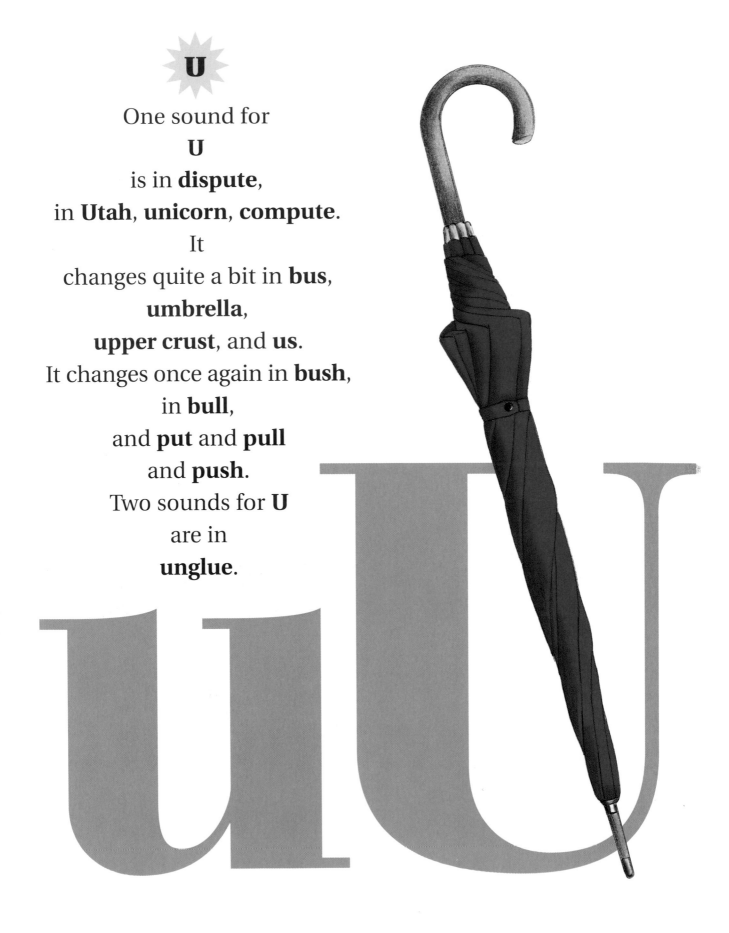

V

We hear
the only sound for **V**
in **river**, **view**, and **victory**,
in **velvet**, **video**, and **vine**,
and
love,
forever,
valentine.

W

The sound for
W
is heard
in
wing and **swing**
and
wow and **word**.
It's
seen
but isn't
heard
in
two,
in **wrinkle**,
wrestle,
wrong,
and
who.

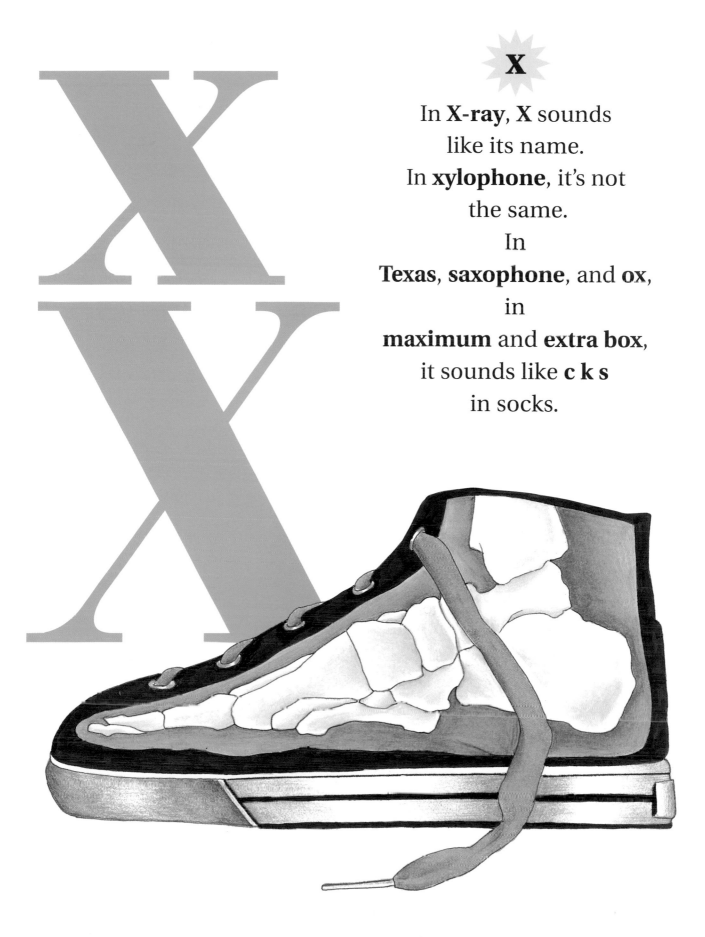

X

In **X-ray**, **X** sounds
like its name.
In **xylophone**, it's not
the same.
In
Texas, **saxophone**, and **ox**,
in
maximum and **extra box**,
it sounds like **c k s**
in socks.

Y

The sound for **Y**
is what we hear
in
yawn and **yoyo**, **yak** and **year**.
In
happily and **fantasy**,
the letter **Y** sounds like an **E**.
It sounds exactly like an **I**
in
fly and **shy** and **type** and **cry**.

 Z
has one sound and one
alone,
as in
zebra, **sizzle**, **zone**,
dazzle, **fuzzy**,
jazz, and **sneeze**,
guzzle, **blizzard**,
lizard, **freeze**.

Addendum means an afterthought
and here are two I'm glad I caught . . .
One for **H** and one for **O**,
information we should know.

H

When **H**'s follow **S** or **C**
or follow **T** or **G** or **P**,
they make the sounds we hear in **share**,
the sounds we hear in **chair** and **there**,
the sound that's at the end of **laugh**,
and at the end of **photograph**.

OO

The double **O**'s we hear
in **zoo**
sound like the **O** we hear
in **who**.
We find those double **O**'s
in **spoon**,
shampoo and **food** and
hoot and **soon**.
They have another sound in
book,
in **cookie**, **foot**, **mistook**, and **look**.
A different sound is found in **poor**,
And other words like **floor** and **door**.
In **blood** and **flood**
they have one more.

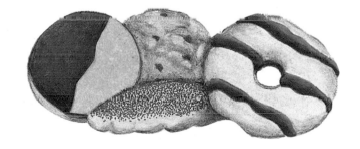